The Player That Every Coach And Club Wants

BY

COACH I. EMEKZ

The player that every coach and club
want.

Copyright © 2022 Coach I. Emekz

DEDICATION

To master Reagan a great sports man and a creative thinker, to Josh mike Coach Johnson without whom this book would have been completed in two years.

TABLE OF CONTENTS

Introduction

Did you know that success doesn't come naturally?

Did you know that behind every greatness there are steps taken? Did you know that success in football is not inborn? The world of football is a very fascinating sector that almost half of the population of human race are interested in it!

There are at least over three million football players in the whole wide world and yet some players have managed to appear in the list of the first hundredth in terms of success to make their names immortals in the world of football. They have distinguished themselves from others, they have proven that one can attain mastery in football, they have shown that there are football players while there are also star amongst them, they have proven that success is attainable in football just as it is in other fields of life.

If there is what I have noticed to be the earnest desire of every footballer whether a kid or an adult, I think it's how to come to limelight and become a great demand in the football market and to become the player that everyone watches and talks about, a player of great relevance and extraordinary talent, a player that coaches would coaches say "get me that boy, I need him in my team."

Football since inception has been operating as a market whereby only those with great qualities or abilities sells and becomes successful in it and this also paints a clear picture of how complicated it is for a player of no quality or ability to find himself in the frontline!

But the question is, why are some players successful and others are not? What is the reason behind these cause and effect? Could it be talent, or could it be luck?

All these have made me to ask myself few questions regarding the reason why some players succeeds while others seem to be buried in the crowed like the majority.

Now, have you asked yourself what is the responsible for this kind of outcome. I wondered, could it be height? But no, I have seen great players of all sizes. I said, could it be from race? But no, I have seen great players from every race so, I was convinced that this has nothing to do with the country you are from and your physique!

I have also wondered could it be that playing in a big club is the reason why some players are successful. but then, I figured out that this has nothing to do with the club you are playing for!

I have watched some players grow and get old without being known as a good player and without achieving anything in their football career. while I have also seen some great players that even at their late thirties are still relevant and still being wanted by great clubs and would be preferred to most young players.

All these left me curious and lead me into a study of why some players succeeds while others don't.

After studying the lives of great players, over a hundred of them that has retained their qualities and relevance for over a decade and also studying other players who I would say they failed, I discovered that success in football doesn't come naturally, and it's not purely about natural talent. The truth is that these two categories of players do things differently. The ones that succeed follows a law while those that fail breaks the law. I found that These laws don't answer to color, size, religion or even age. It works for consistent practitioners. Interestingly, anyone who cares to follow these laws will achieve similar results in terms of success. It doesn't matter if you came from a country that no one has ever played football before, it doesn't matter if you came from a poor background, the only barrier here would be willingness to follow these discovered steps. These laws are not selective. It doesn't care about the person practicing it, all it cares about is to deliver the results anywhere the processes are followed.

It is said that success is systematic, and it leaves a track and can also be replicated if one can find the track of any successful person that he wants to be like and follow the same track he will eventually achieve the same results.

I have seen ordinary players turn to stars just by following these steps. But just before you start reading this book, I'd like you to decide or think about the type of player you would like the world to see you as.

Could it be the best midfielder in the world?

Could it be the best central defender in the world?

Could it be the best striker in the world?

Or the best goalkeeper?

It doesn't matter what your choice are, it is attainable! Best players in the world are not superhuman, they weren't born stars, even though some individuals are born with great abilities but, I can tell you that this success has little or nothing to do with that! And the truth remains that no matter how precious your abilities are, if it is not developed, you will not see its beauty.

In the quest to study what leads to success and failure in football, I discovered that success is methodological; it is instruction-based and has nothing to do with luck!

This book unveils what makes a great player and what you what makes some people to fail in their football career.

Just a word of instruction before we go into the quest for greatness. I want you to make up your mind to do whatever it takes to do as guided in this book, not just for the first week after reading this book rather, all the days of your playing career.

The prove that you have read this book, is when you put the instructions to action, not just for one year but to make it a lifestyle until you become a player of relevance, a player that your teammates, coaches, club, or your country will be proud of and at the end, you will achieve happiness, fulfilment, and wealth as a reward!

Chapter one

Things that make some players to fail

One of the mind-blowing facts about life is, you don't need to do many things to fall, all you need is, leave yourself and you will fall like a tree but, that is contrary to what it takes to rise. If you want to stand up, you will need to set your hands and legs properly and apply force and energy before you stand. This tells us that rising in life does not come naturally, it requires some steps!

In my little journey in life, I have always wondered why some players became successful while others don't. Like, it's just few players that succeeds, why is it so? Well, from my findings and experience as a formal goalkeeper, I have discovered that these few things listed beneath are the core reasons responsible for the reason why players fail or succeeds, and they are what distinguishes the successful from the unsuccessful.

Mindset

There is nothing that makes or breaks a person like mindset. What is mindset? It is a person's way of thinking or a set of assumptions. Just as every software functions the way they are programed, every living being live as a reflection of their mindset. The mindset of players that succeeds and the one that doesn't are not the same thing. They have different mindset; they have different assumptions about success. The set of players that fails believes that success is something that happens naturally and sees others who succeed as those that are gifted by nature to do well. They don't see success as something you can achieve if you are not talented, and they see others who succeed as those that are favored by nature.

The don't see success as something that comes as a result of our actions. To them if it is not flowing naturally, you can't have it and as a result of that they don't bother to go extra mile in their training. They see success as something that is inborn.

Then the other type of players which are the category of players that succeeds has growth mindset. Believes that success comes through learning and hard work. They believe that they can develop any skill that that they lack. They focus on their personal improvement; they see themselves solely responsible for the outcome of their lives. So, to them, in order to achieve what they want, the go extra in thinking, training and planning just to get their goals.

Lack of vision or dream

It is said that those that succeeds in business are those that has a clear and specific vision. Seriously, I think that this rule applies to anything you want to succeed in life! I found that players who doesn't succeed are never had a vision. They never wanted to be best of something. They just play because they are footballers. They didn't have an aim, there was nothing pushing them to do something beyond their normal. They didn't have what they wanted to achieve badly!

They lacked what to become and therefore there is nothing left but ordinary.

Ignorance

It is said that ignorance is worse than blindness. When I was at the age of 11, I didn't know how to read, I was what they call a dummy. This was because I lost my mom when I can barely talk and her mum who doesn't know how to read and write took me, I didn't start schooling like most kids, and any day she looked me she gets pissed off, so, I always feel bad, and I don't know why but that was a fact.

I knew I was a smart kid but everyone else knows me as a dummy because I don't how to read. So, one day, I decided to ask someone who I always see reading.

I said to him, excuse me, may I ask you a question, he said, yea! I asked him, "how does people read, is it something you are born with? For a second, he looked at me astonishingly and said, 'no. He continued, everybody learnt how to read, nobody was born with that ability to read. We all learnt it.' I said, wow!" It was as if a scale fell off my eyes!

So, from that day, I took it upon myself to learn how to read, and believe me, that was a breakthrough for me.

Also in football, some players don't know how that greatness or success in football isn't inborn or natural. They think that those who succeeds or play well, are born to do so, not knowing that it's not it.

The ignorance here is that they don't know that every player both the ones we see as a great player and they ones that nobody would recommend all came to this world as a blank canvas. But they developed themselves into what you now see them as.

Talent can either come naturally or it can be developed, just as we learn to read you can also learn to play. You can learn to become any type of player that you want.

Chapter two

Dreams Gives Birth To Reality

One of the life lessons that I am grateful of today is that no one arrives at a future he cannot see. This is because, if you don't know what you are looking for, you can't recognize it when you see it. Vision or a dream in this context is not the dream of the night rather, it is the future that you see of yourself with your imagination of your tomorrow you can see this even when your eyes are closed.

When I was a kid, I went to a seminar, in which the man who taught on that event left me with a food for the thought. He said, "the greatest nation is imagination. All of the things we see in existence today all came from imagination. They were had as a dream before coming to reality.

Dreams or vision originates from imagination; this is not wishing! It is a process of engaging your mind in creating what can be achieved.

So, what is imagination? It is the ability to form mental pictures or images of something that is not perceived through your five senses.

This is what I found that great players do, they try to see tomorrow with their imaginative faculty, they imagine themselves being a high performer and they work at bringing it to reality. They imagine themselves, being they best and they create what you see them as with their mind.

Every Football player is talented but not everyone of is successful. That is to tell you that Talent only does guarantee success, there are other ingredients you need to mix with talent as a footballer to see your career well flavored, and number one is, you must have a vision!

Now, here is another point, having just a dream is not the ultimate because when a dream is not channeled towards problem solving, it makes no sense. Having a dream is not enough to make you a player that every coach wants. You must be a problem-solving player. You must endeavor to find a particular problem you will solve with your dream. This is the first step; it doesn't matter whether you have the talent to solve the problem now or not, just discover a problem you want to solve. It is proven that talents can come from two means: inborn or developed through hard work.

In my early days as a teenager who plays for a club, I was a goalkeeper. Before I joined the club, they had two goalkeepers, but before I came to the club, I already know that no matter how many people who are there before me, I know that the role of a goalkeeper is to stop the ball from getting into the net, and I have already seen that most goalkeepers believes that some balls are meant to go into the net and no matter what you do you can't stop it. So, I knew that was a limiting believe. And it's a problem as well, because you are meant to stop the ball from getting into the net. So, I used that as an advantage, I said to myself, "if I can stop those unstoppable balls from getting into the net, with time I could be the number one!

So, I began to train my mind and body by making it possible first in my mind and watching other great saves from other goalkeepers. I studied their errors and used it as my competitive advantage. After a while of training hard and learning how to move my body with speed with my mind, the day that an opportunity was given to me on a match as a second goalkeeper, I never returned as a second keeper. And this all started with identifying a problem and then building my dream around it.

When you look at the world of football today, you can see that 80% of players are visionless. They don't improve from year to year. When you operate by vision, you must continually improve and by so doing you can never be displaced. You can never be a benchwarmer, rather you will be improving day by day because you are continuously working to be better and therefore Your relevance will make you a star.

But what type of player is every coach looking for?

Some coaches that I met has made it known that they are looking for the kind of player that is always in every match, the player that fills in the gap of his position. I guess that is something that is achievable?
here is what they mean by being a player to fills the gap of his position: it is being a player that won't be in a match, and yet a need for his position or role will still be alarming. So, if you want to be a striker, discover what makes strikers good or bad; they quality that a striker would lack, and he will be classified as a bad striker. Find out what coaches complain of those strikers that are not good. It could be positioning (that is, being at the right place at the right time), it could be making the right moves, it could be scoring impossible goals or scoring when no one expects.

So, you must observe all these and be good at other people's mistake.

At my early days, I hear people make all manner of excuses why they missed the ball while I was busy building strength from their mistakes.

So, you must ask yourself this question, what type of player do I want to be? Is it the best midfielder in the world? Your dream must be able to answer it.

This is where it starts from, you must identify the gap you want to fill or occupy!

Here are few steps to take after the dream has been conceived.

Discover what others are getting wrong.

The reason clubs buy players is nothing but to fill in a gab or stop a leakage. In business, if you want to be better than others, then you must counter them at their flaws. Great players learn to build strength in what others considers as a weakness. Discover what makes others bad; what makes others good but not good enough and make it your area of concentration.

If You want to be a defensive midfielder, you must learn how to dispossess your opponent within the midfield zone or anywhere. You must not let them perform that's one of your duties. The reason why some coaches buy midfield players even when they have one is because their own midfielders are always outperformed by their opponents.

If you want to be a defender, you must learn how to be able to find out what makes others bad and use it as your strength. I know the dream of every coach is to have that defender the no one crosses. If you want to be a goalkeeper, be a goalkeeper that won't let any ball get into the net no matter what.

Every coach wants the best, and the way to becoming the best is by doing the best.

I was able to outshine the number one during my time as a goalkeeper because I discovered a weakness that almost every goalkeeper had and made sure that I am the most improved and by doing that, I was ahead of them.

Learn To Fill The Gap

Now, after finding out the faults of others, it doesn't matter even if they are not in the same team with you. You can make explorative research on the midfield players If that's what you want to be and highlight all those that are doing well and others that are not doing well, and ask yourself, what makes these ones very good and what makes these ones to be lost in the crowed?

Well, like I said earlier in the book that what makes some players succeeds is because they obey laws, while others that fails breaks it. Football is like a business that if you must be greater than your competitors then you must be better than them in everything.

So, how do you fill in the gap:

- **Acquire the missing ability or skill that is not in other players.**

Now, if you find yourself in a situation whereby everyone, you'd like to take their place are better than you, then you must work harder than them for you to take their place. This is possible through specific trainings. This is not the training you do with your other teammates to keep fit. This is training you personally engage yourself with in order to acquire certain qualities. This is one of the things those great players do, they spent more time on personal training than others. They work on improving, those areas that others flop at. Acquiring the missing ability might be just learning how to attack your opponent or how to win tackles, it might be how to play accurate passes, it might be how to shoot on target from afar.

In football, nothing just happens without practice.

It might be how to dribble. I have seen some players desire to be a very good dribbler, but they don't know how to go about it.

Dribbling can be done in two ways:

By skill or by dodging!

I will use two players who are popular as an example. For instance, Messi and Neymar. Neymar is more skillful and that's what he uses in dribbling people while Messi is good with dodging, he doesn't do show much skill like Neymar, but he knows how to avoid his opponents whenever he is with the ball.

They all attained these qualities by learning and practicing.

How does learn come in football?

Learning comes through observation and practicing. Whatever you want to learn in football, you must spend time watching others who knows how to do what you want to learn and practice it too.

• Observe and out-train.

After observing others who does what you want to learn very well, the next thing is to practice and train to be better than them.

One of my problems with those who have what I can idle is that they only practice or train to be like their idles, they don't aspire to be greater. But My question has always been, what is the need of being a counterfeit of another person?

Now, if others train two hours a day, you must train three! Make yourself to be so hard to beat.

Out-train your competitors and outwork them on the pitch. There is a saying I love so much, it says, "hard work can take you where talent fails."

• Master the art

I am a very good fan of success and I study every successful individual that grabs my attention. In my quest for success, I have discovered through observation that success comes through mastery and that those that are successful at any field of endeavors are those that have attained mastery in that field.

Mastery is attaining high level of skill or professionalism through learning, practicing and experience. Mastery in football is becoming the best at what you do. It is a phase in your career where you are full of excellence. It is a phase that the tendency of making mistakes is less than 20%. It is not that there will never be a mistake there will be but it's going to be limited and most times they will be covered by your excellence.

Football is an art, it can be learned and mastered, it can be learned from those who play professionally just by watching them and practicing what you are seeing.

What I want you to know is that nobody was born a professional footballer. We were only born with the talent and in some cases, natural interest!

Just like nobody is born a reader, but you learn it. That's how nobody was born a professional footballer, people learn everything that they display on the pitch on the training ground.

Those players you see that everyone is talking about, spend quality time in train and working on themselves, and learning from their errors. It is hard for you to become that which you dream of becoming if all you do is to train the way others train and sleep when they sleep. You must aim to add extra effort every day.

Those little tricks and skills in football that you desire can be learned if you can spend quality time alone, thinking, analyzing, and practicing! It is what you learnt in your closet that you display on the training ground, and it is what you learnt on the training ground that you display on the match day.

Here is how to attain mastery in football

- ## Discover what you lack and what you need.

For me, when I was starting up as a goalkeeper, I discovered that I lacked speed. As a goalkeeper, my response time was poor (that is not having enough speed that can equal and can enable me to catch any ball that I want). And I know that if I can improve on this fault my life will be 70% improved. So, I did just that and my life was greatly improved.

Your fault as a young player might be lack of ball control or making lots of inaccurate passes or scoring problem or as a striker you don't know how to position yourself or make right moves. As a player who dreams to attain mastery in football, your first duty is to discover where your shortcoming is coming from and once this is discovered, the next thing is to correct it.

A time came in my life as a goalkeeper that I discovered that most goalkeepers dive on guesses when it comes to catching penalties. One day I said to myself, can't anything be done on this?

So, I began to think of how I can stop diving on guesses rather diving on purpose. So, after analyzing several penalties, I discovered that most goalkeepers focus on the eyes of the penalty taker, or they focus on the body movement and leg instead of focusing on the ball.

So, I started focusing my eyes on ball and improving my response speed in order to follow any ball that is played with the same intensity, after a while of training and practicing, I became very good with catching penalties. And funny enough most people started to think and say that I am gifted with catching penalties not knowing that a great work has been done outside the pitch to enable those performances and by doing so, I distinguished myself from other goalkeepers.

So, identify what has been the cause of downtime in your football career and improve greatly on it so that it will no longer be a fault but a selling point. A player who will attain mastery must continually improve in all his weaknesses.

• Give 101% of yourself

Both in the training ground and on a match day, withhold nothing! Give everything, let your whole body, mind, and strength be involved in whatever you do on the pitch. Players who become great are the ones who give their all and all, see yourself as the livewire of your team. Be a workaholic player; see it as part of serving with your purpose. Don't let the lack of involvement, or weaknesses of others affect you. Just go ahead and be a workaholic

By giving your 101%, mind you, don't allow your opponent to perform on the pitch, and when the ball gets to your leg turn around with confidence and give an accurate passing without mistakes.

You can never see a lazy player who is a star. Putting an average effort in your football career will make you an average player, while putting a great amount of effort will make you a highflier!

Make it a promise to yourself that you are going to be a workaholic player and when you are on the pitch and feel like getting tired remind yourself the promise you made to yourself and just say boldly, "this is the life I have chosen, it's a price I must pay to become what I want to be"

• Undergo apprenticeship

Ronaldinho of Brazil, one of the most skillful footballers during his time as a player once said, "I learnt from Jay-Jay Okocha."

This is to prove that mastery requires apprenticeship, you need to spend time watching those players you admire or aspire to be like and learn from them. Nowadays, their physical presence doesn't even matter, you can stay in your room and watch any player you want through the internet.

Everything you see people display on the pitch all came through learning and practicing. It's not magic or the matter of being a genius, it is learnt. And anything you want is learnable, it will only take time and determination. And what you need to know about taking steps is that "nothing works for the first time. In most cases it might work on the tenth time, it might take lesser than that or it might take longer than that so, don't give up too soon! Most people who have attained mastery in their field failed many times before they grew to perfection.

Take the process of apprenticeship very serious, see it as though you are writing a school exam, be conscientious about it; always know you are working for a purpose and focus in developing yourself.

Chapter three

Great Players Are Hard workers

I have a simple formula that I look unto, I apply it in everything in my life and it works for me, I believe it will be of help to you:

Talent + effort = skill

Skill + effort = achievement

I believe that if you remove effort from anything that you do, you will achieve nothing! But, how about you decide to add extra 50% hard work to your playing career? You will have greater results than you have ever had before.

Hard work is the only way to avoid hard life, and interestingly, it does not kill, it's a kind of painful but it beautifies! Sports like football requires great amount input in labor if you must stand out from the crowed.

How about you become the guy that everyone will say, if not for you we would have lost this match, or the one that everyone would say, we won because of you. And how about you do that same thing every day in every match?

Success is not a once and for all event, it is making progress continually. I have watched many matches just for observation's sake, and I found that 80% of the time, the man that wins the man of the match is always as a result of great input.

When I was a goalkeeper, I keep like as if I don't have defenders. Putting normal effort or energy will only make you to be like every other player on the pitch, and of course I know you want to stand out! Playing like a rich man won't allow the star in you to shine, rather playing like a slave will do that. You can outshine any player you want by going beyond your normal or the normal. Mastery backed with hard work is nothing but success unstoppable. If you must be the player that every coach wants, then you must be a hard worker.

Here is a tip that will help you. Whenever you are playing in a match, no matter your position, don't allow your direct opponent to perform no matter who they, when you bare this in mind and make it your aim, you will then have a reason to work hard. And don't look at others before you contribute, just work hard as though you are the only one on the pitch. Involve your whole being, don't withhold your zeal because others are underperforming, doing that will only shade your stardom instead, be the only player that it will be said that despite the weakness of this club, this guy played well.

Outshine everyone by your work rate, both your team members and your opponents. And don't do this because you want to be praised, rather, do it as what you ought to do to separate yourself from others and remember, life is not a race of majority rather, a race of individuality. Promotions and increase in wages don't come to everybody at the same time, it occurs individually.

Hard work is what determines your relevance and worth. Hard workers don't stay on the bench, they always have a game time, unless they are tired or injured, their contribution to any team won't let any coach to keep them on the bench.

So, if you must be a great player, one of the things you must love is hard work. Just hate to be known as a normal player, be the rock that holds your team. Be the one that everyone would say I wish I can play like him. one of the things you must bear in mind as a player who wants to be great is that there is no substitute for hard work as long as football is concerned.

How do you work hard as a player?

- **You must decide to do so and commit to doing it.**

Decision is really a solid way to condition the mind and the body to act or behave a certain way. One of the areas you can see decision in action is in marriage. Love in marriage is a decision-based thing, it is your decision to love your partner that will still make you to be in love even when it seems like all emotions are washed away, when it seems like that the beauty that you once saw has faded away, it is decision to that keeps you going at such times.

Decision is the language of discipline. So, if you must be that hard working player you must decide to do so; this is because sometimes and somewhere in the middle, you will not feel like to work, but at such time, it's time to remind yourself that it is your decision to work hard, when you remember that it is your decision and choice, you will see great strength that you can't see where it is coming from and willpower that will saturate your being and help you to push on.

• You must train and practice hard

You can only manifest what you have practiced! If you train or practice with intensity, then it will be easier for you to replicate the same thing on the match day. There is a saying which says, "you don't learn how to shoot on a battlefield" in other words, performing great on a match day must find its origin on the training ground.

- ## Set goals to work hard.

Did you know that if you must achieve anything that is worthwhile, you must set a goal on it?

Setting a goal helps you to measure your improvement on anything, it helps you to track your progress, and not only that but, it also helps you to channel your effort towards your aim. So, just before you step out to train and practice, sit down and write your goals, write down how many hours you'd train per day, write down the specific training or practice you'd involve yourself in on daily basis. That's the way to go! The most important thing about goals is, it must be time-bounded, this is the only thing that makes a goal. You must know and decide what to achieve within a set time else, it wouldn't be called a goal. Goals enforces us to be prompt, and that's what helps us to achieve our aim.

- ## Plan to become better everyday

Highly successful players make sure that they are not at the same level every day, they make sure that no day ends where the previous ended.

Great players, makes sure that there is an improvement daily on their training and on the match day. They are high performers. Set your everyday goals to be a bit improve every day. For instance, if your work rate is 34% today, make sure that by tomorrow it is 40% and that's how you can grow from good to better and from better to best.

Chapter four

Consistency Is The Soul Of Progress

A player that every coach would want must be a consistent and persistent player. This is one the qualities found in great players. They are not just seasonal! They are good in season and out of the season.

One of the things that most great clubs check before signing a player is, they check his consistency record, and this is to show you how important it is. If you lack consistency in your career success might be a bit far from you.

Don't be like most players who believes that things just happen on its own, don't be like the majority who thinks that good performance just happens as a result of talent or luck. Things doesn't happen like that, especially in football. It is actions that triggers results.

To maintain consistency, you must train and prepare consistently and don't see any match as a small match, see every match as a big match, see every day as a day to do your best. Be fervent always both in the training ground and on the real match. Some players seem to use different energy or zeal according to the team they are facing, and this is what makes players to have fluctuations in their performances.

Consistency in this context is maintaining the same intensity, work rate and commitment both when season just kicked off, midseason and end of the season. It is having a track a record. Performing greatly in the beginning of the season is not just what will make you a great player. You must make sure that your yesterday is not better than your today in every match all through the season.

Simple ways to maintain consistency in your performance

- **Stick to your goal.**

    One of the great advantages of having a goal is, it helps us to live a well guided life. Doing according to what is in your goal will mean a lot to your goal every day. Goals helps us to improve on our dreams, and following your goals makes success to be lot easier.

- **Keep renewing your commitment**

Sticking to a goal is sometimes difficult and requires great amount of discipline to maintain especially if you are not used to following goals. When you come to a situation whereby you feel like you are off from your goal. Then, it is a very good moment to renew your commitment to your goals again. Try to remind yourself about what you are aiming to achieve, and what it will mean to your career if you can only get back on the track.

Chapter five

Be a confident player

Players that every coach would want are players of great confidence. They are the players that when they are with the ball, you will see great composure at work in them and which is the number one quality of anybody who has attained mastery in his field. A striker with great confidence, when he is faced with the goalkeeper, will not play the ball out of fear and tension but will make sure he puts the ball where the goalkeeper will not be able to catch it.

When you see average players, it is easier for you to see lack of self-confidence in them. You would see, it if he is a striker, you will see it in his positioning, or in the way of attacking or if he is a goalkeeper, you would see it in the way he keeps.

what causes lack of self-confidence?

Let's look at the things found responsible for lack of confidence in players.

- **Lack of mastery:**

Mastery is being good at what you do, it is attaining excellence in your field of endeavor. Now, here is a great question, have you seen anybody who knows how to cook at a professional level and still feel incompetent when cooking in his home?

Have you seen a 10yrs old kid who knows how to walk but displays lack of self-confidence in walking? I know the answer is no, this is to tell you that you will always have confidence for whatever you know how to do it.

Lack of confidence in anything means you have not mastered the art; you have not learnt the rhythm.

So, the cure to lack of confidence as a player is to know how to do what you are known for. Develop and master the skills of playing in your position or role. For instance, if you are a striker, have all the qualities of a good striker. And you will see that you have nothing to fear. If you are a defender know how to stop attacks, know how to win area battles, know how to make the right moves, be a "No Go Area" defender in order words be a defender that is too hard for any opponent to pass through, be a defender that owns his box, a defender that won't let any ball cross him or get to the goalkeeper.

• The fear of failure

The fear of failure is the single greatest human obstacle to growth and success. It retards success, it stops you from trying or going beyond your normal.

But what is this fear of failure?

It is the fear of what you think people will think of you if you fail or make great mistakes over a given task.

I always tell people that this fear is just an anticipation of what might happen if some thing should go wrong. I always tell them that what you are scared of has not happened yet, its object is failure, and failure can only occur if we fail to do what we are supposed to do over a given task. For instance, if you want to fail your exams in school, don't read. So, if you are a student in this situation, how to terminate that fear is by reading, and getting so prepared. The fear of failure comes when we think we are not yet ready or much prepared to do something, it always focuses on your weaknesses.

Now, if you want to overcome this fear you must identify the object of this fear and kill it by preparing for that which causes you to fear.

So, as a player whom the crowed would come out and watch, the easiest way to terminate the fear of failure, is becoming better in your weaknesses. Learn those things you are scared that you might make mistake on. Perfect in them.

Fear of failure is not a living being, it is just an anticipation of bad performance.

Here is my little technique of overcoming the fear of failure. The fear of failure only comes when you know you are not good at thing which you want to do and you don't want people to know that you are not good at this, you don't want to feel embarrassed.

So, the way to overcome this fear is to focus on becoming good at what you are not good at. Become so good at it you will see that the fear will vanish! This is because, no one is scared of what he or she is good at.

- **Inferiority complex**

This is one the problems found in most players, both at the professional level and at the local level. They believe that other players who plays well or have a unique and a superior quality and are more gifted by nature than them. So, as a result of this, they have adopted the mindset of "I AM NOT AS TALENTED" most players feel like what they possess is inferior talent, they don't really have faith in their own uniqueness. They feel untalented, they feel like they are fake while those who plays well are supreme.

Here's my advice on this. Talent can either be inborn or developed, so you have nothing to feel inferior about. It's not a matter of talent, it's about cultivation, it about the level commitment you are willing to give in order to develop your talent. talents are just like raw material; it requires development and that's what decides how colorful it will ever be. They reason why you see those players that do excellently well is because they have cultivated their talents.

Nobody was born already great or greater than each other naturally. It is our actions, choices and belief that makes us who we are.

Printed in Great Britain
by Amazon

10222534R00031